'The Mighty Warrior' Prayers for Seasons like these

'I will lift up mine eyes unto the hills, from whence cometh my help. My help cometh from the LORD, which made heaven and earth.' Psalm 121:1, 2.

Sometimes in life, when the unexpected happens, we are distraught. We seek for words to express our disillusionments, we try to discern our needs, and what to ask for in prayer. These prayers, are for moments like these. In crisis situations, prayers could be the only Lifeline! Take time to talk with God. Simple prayers yield incredible Outcomes. They dislodge mountains even to this day. In this book, there

1

are accompanying Bible verses with each prayer and thanksgiving, to help guide you through each category of need you may have. It is reassuring to know that God hears and answers prayers. May the Lord hear you when you call. Amen.

'I called upon the LORD in distress: the LORD answered me, *and set me* in a large place.' Psalm 118:5.

'This poor man cried, and the LORD heard *him*, and saved him out of all his troubles.' Psalm 34:6.

CONTENTS   PAGES

Prayer for Daily Provision

IT IS WRITTEN

'The Lord is my Shepherd; I shall not want.' Psalm 23:1.

'I have been young, and now am old; yet have I not seen the righteous forsaken, nor his seed begging bread.' Psalm 37:25.

'For ye know the grace of our Lord Jesus Christ, that, though he was rich, yet for your sakes he became poor, that ye through his poverty might be rich.' 2 Corinthians 8:9.

MY PRAYER

Lord, I ask for Your commanded blessings upon my life in Jesus Name

I pray for a financial breakthrough.

You *stripped* the Syrians of their possessions and passed them on to Your chosen ones, Israel in Samaria. Overnight, You made the poor, rich by Your Divine instrumentation. You are unfathomable.

Activate this Divine transference of wealth into my life, which is according to Your Word, that the wealth of the wicked is laid up for the righteous.

Let rivers flow in this wilderness. Turn this desert into an Oasis of Wealth. The Silver and Gold, are Yours, the Power to create wealth is given by You.

You are the God of Increase. I ask for exponential increase, multiplicity of wealth which You covenanted to Abraham with optimised favour.

Realign me with wealth, with Divine Contacts and associations, I pray in Jesus Name. Amen.

PROMULGATIONS

Every need is met, every bill is paid in the Name of Jesus.

Every debt is paid, every lack is nullified in Jesus Name.

Whom God has blessed; no man can curse. God's seal of Approval is upon my life. It is solidified and cannot be revoked in Jesus Name. Amen.

I claim my divine inheritance in Jesus Name. Amen.

I possess my possessions.

Faith in Jesus is my <u>Divine Currency</u>.

THANKSGIVING

Thank You Lord, I receive great provision and abundant supplies of all my needs according to Your riches in glory through Christ Jesus. I shall lack no good thing. Amen.

Jesus is the Bread of life. None satisfies but Him!

PRAISE NOTES

_____

_____

_____

_____

_____

_____

_____

_____

_____

_____

_____

_____

_____

_____

_____

Prayer for Promotion

IT IS WRITTEN

'He raiseth up the poor out of the dust, *and* lifteth the needy out of the dunghill; That he may set *him* with princes, *even* with the princes of his people.' Psalm 113:7, 8.

'For promotion *cometh* neither from the east, nor from the west, nor from the south.' Psalm 75:6.

PAPA! ABBA FATHER!

Only You can save.

Only You can bless, and it is blessed.

Only You can make rich and it adds no sorrow with it.

Raise me up above mine contenders.

Set me up above every limitation.

The power to *elevate* and to *relegate* is in Your Hands.

You put one down, and You raise up the other.

All Power belongs to You Lord.

Make me the head and not the tail, above only and not beneath, according to Your Word.

Promotion *comes neither* from the east, nor from the west, nor from the south but from You.

I have put my trust in You and will serve You alone.

In Jesus Name. Amen.

PROMULGATIONS

I decree advancements.

I declare Affluence and Influence

I recover lost grounds; the years the enemy had embezzled

By God, I overturn every wicked plot of the enemy

By God I leap over every wall, and hinderances on my path

I disallow whatever had been imposed on me, to my disadvantage

I mount up with wings as an eagle

The blessings of God on my life and my family, are irreversible and uncontainable!

I impose God's sanctions upon my enemies. I revoke every scheme and plot of the wicked against me.

I authorise God's judgements through the Blood of Jesus.

I invoke God's Power and Authority over my life, and my family.

Christ has blotted out every handwriting of ordinance that was against God's Divine destiny for me and my family by His precious Blood.

For if God be for me. Who can be against me?

Nothing shall by any means hurt me

God is my *Defence!*

I declare that *THIS IS A NEW DAY!*

I overcome by the *Blood* of the *Lamb* and by the *Word* of my testimony that *Jesus Christ Is Lord* of my life. *Amen.*

THANKSGIVING

Thank You Lord for you have heard me. Thank You Lord. 'He hath put down the mighty from *their* seats, and exalted them of low degree.' Luke 1:52

Jesus said, I have come to give you life, and life more abundantly.

PRAISE NOTES

_____

_____

_____

_____

_____

_____

_____

_____

_____

_____

_____

_____

_____

Prayer for Confidence in God

IT IS WRITTEN

'Let not your heart be troubled: ye believe in God, believe also in me.' John 14:1.

'In the world ye shall have tribulation: but be of good cheer; I have overcome the world.' John 16:33c.

'Rejoice not against me, O mine enemy: when I fall, I shall arise; when I sit in darkness, the LORD shall be a light unto me.' Micah 7:8.

MY PRAYER

Lord show forth your Power. Win this battle for me.

Erase every disquietness and doubt in my heart.

Set my confidence in You Alone.

The psalmist said, '*I had fainted*, unless I had believed to see the goodness of the *LORD* in the land of the living.' Psalm 27:13.

Destroy every arrow of doubt the enemy has sent against me, to antagonise me.

In quietness and in confidence, shall be my strength.

Demobilise and *destabilise* my enemies,

Undo their works, for my hope is in You O Lord! I pray in the Mighty Name of Jesus. Amen.

PROMULGATIONS

Every arrow of the wicked against my mind, my thoughts are broken in Jesus Name.

I silence every voice of intimidation

I bind every lying spirit in the Name of Jesus

I arrest and lay captive every thought and dominion to the Obedience of Christ

I relegate all demonic operation into their fallen estate

I declare that you are subjugated to God's power and authority in my life

I disband your operations in my life in Jesus Name

The Blood of Jesus advocates for me

'The Lord on High is mightier than the noise of many waters; yea than the mighty waves of the sea.' Psalm 93:4.

THANKSGIVING

Thank you, Lord, for answered prayers. I overcome every doubt and unbelief, every worry and anxiety, every fear and intimidation, through the Blood of Jesus. Thank You Lord, for Your presence. My confidence is in You. 'It *is* better to trust in the LORD than to put confidence in man.' Psalm 118:8.

Jesus is the Author and Finisher
of my faith.

PRAISE NOTES

_____
_____
_____
_____
_____
_____
_____
_____
_____
_____
_____
_____
_____
_____
_____
_____
_____

Prayer Against Insecurity

IT IS WRITTEN

'Can a woman forget her sucking child, that she should not have compassion on the son of her womb? yea, they may forget, yet will I not forget thee.' Isaiah 49:15

'I will never leave thee, nor forsake thee.' Hebrews 13:5c.

MY PRAYER

Lord teach me to abide in Your Love

Help me to tabernacle in Your presence, in the comfort of Your Spirit and in the power of Your love.

Stabilise my faith

Instruct my emotions

Mobilise me by the truth of your Word which says that I am blessed;

Highly Favoured;

Never forgotten nor Forsaken;

not rejected or disowned but chosen

And loved by You, with an everlasting love.

Impart these truths into my heart

Help me to *internalise them*

Help me to know that I am the beloved of the Lord, and the Apple of His Eyes in Jesus Name. Amen!

PROMULGATIONS

I am blessed

I am His beloved

God delights in me

Therefore, I shall not be moved

For, the righteous shall be as mount Zion

that cannot be shaken

Nothing shall be able to separate me from the

love of Christ

For I know whom I have believed and I am

persuaded that He is able to preserve that

which I have committed unto Him against that

day.

I am saved by the Blood of Jesus

I am sealed by the love of Christ

Beneath are His everlasting Arms.

The LORD will perfect all *which* concerns
me.

THANKSGIVING

Lord, I receive your unconditional Love and healing in Jesus Name. Amen.

Greater love hath no man than this; Jesus laid

down his life for me.

Thank You Lord!

PRAISE NOTES

_____

_____

_____

_____

_____

_____

_____

_____

_____

_____

_____

_____

_____

_____

_____

_____

Prayer for Healing

IT IS WRITTEN

'I will put none of these diseases upon thee, which I have brought upon the Egyptians: <u>for I am the LORD that healeth thee.</u>' Exodus 15:26c.

'Bless the LORD, O my soul, and forget not all his benefits: Who forgiveth all thine iniquities; who healeth all thy diseases;'.

Psalm 103:2,3.

MY PRAYER

Heal me O Lord!

Send shock waves of Your healing power through my body. Surround me with Your Fire!

Strengthen my bones

Enable me to do those things, which I could not do before in Jesus Name

Normalise every chemical imbalance

Realign every misalignment

Optimise my immunity

Saturate my body with Your Holy Presence

Power of the Living God, fall afresh on me!

PROMULGATIONS

J command *normality* on my entire body in the Name of *J*esus.

J command every cell, every nerve, my flesh, my bones, every tissue of my body to realign its functionality to God's intentional purpose

J command every pain and sickness to *dissipate* in *J*esus Name.

Spirit of the living God, radiate through this body

Quicken these mortal frames

J summons every spirit of infirmity operating in this body:

Every yoke of pain, fever, tumor, viruses, any
abnormality,

I curse your roots in the Mighty Name of
Jesus

I discharge you out from this body right now,
in the Name of Jesus

I arraign you before the judgement seat of God
Eternal.

I am healed!

My body is the temple of the Living God; the
temple of the Holy Spirit. Amen!

THANKSGIVING

I will praise thee for I am fearfully and wonderfully made: marvellous are thy works; and that my soul knoweth right well.' Psalm 139:14. Lord I receive Your healing. My health is restored. I have seen Your mercies and loving kindnesses toward me. May the

Lord be glorified. May God alone be magnified. Jehovah Rapha!

Surely Jesus hath borne my griefs, and carried away my sorrows.

PRAISE NOTES

_____
_____
_____
_____
_____
_____
_____
_____
_____
_____
_____
_____

Prayer for When Afraid

IT IS WRITTEN

'The LORD is on my side; I will not fear: what can man do unto me?' Psalm 118:6.

'Fear thou not; for I am with thee: be not dismayed; for I am thy God: I will strengthen thee; yea, I will help thee; yea, I will uphold thee with the right hand of my righteousness.' Isaiah 41:10.

MY PRAYER

Lord please be with me.

Send Your comfort to my soul.

Take away the spirit of fear and fill me with Your power.

Grant me boldness before my enemies.

Speak Your words into my heart, that will dispel every fear.

I immerse myself into the love and the power of Christ.

I bind and cast out the spirit of fear in the Name of Jesus. God has not given me the spirit of fear, but of power, and of love and of a Sound mind.

PROMULGATIONS

I dispossess myself from the spirit of fear

I cast down every imagination,

I cast down every hierarchy of the wicked one;

I cast down every high thing which exalts itself above the knowledge of the *Living God*

I reassign you to your destruction

I counter every negative thought with the *Word* of God that:

No weapon formed against me shall ever prosper

Greater is *He* that is in me than he that is in the world.

He is near that justifieth me, who shall contend with me?

'Though an host should encamp against me, my heart shall not fear: though war should arise against me, in this will I be confident.' Psalm 27:3.

THANKSGIVING

Thank You Lord for your presence. Thank You Lord for You have heard my prayers. I receive the divine nature of Christ. I receive God's power, love and a Sound mind; a life without fear in the Mighty Name of Jesus. I am as Bold as a Lion. Amen.

Jesus is the Lion of the Tribe of Judah.

PRAISE NOTES

Prayer when Seeking for Direction

IT IS WRITTEN

'I will instruct thee and teach thee in the way which thou shalt go: I will guide thee with mine eye.' Psalm 32:8.

'In all thy ways acknowledge him, and he shall direct thy paths.' Proverbs 3:6.

MY PRAYER

Lord show me the way to go.

Direct my thoughts and conversations aright, that they might bring about a profitable and expected outcome for Your glory.

Take away carnality and worldly wisdom of men Give to me, Your wisdom.

Wisdom that will bring peace, for the wisdom from above promotes peace.

Give to me, wisdom that will save lives as You gave to Solomon.

Give me Wisdom in rightly appropriating the divine Counsel of God, in Jesus Name.

Establish my path.

Reveal truth to me.

Open mine eyes to any pitfalls the enemy might have hidden on my path and guide me safely through.

Lead me not into temptation but deliver me from every evil in Jesus Name.

Manoeuvre me into the right path.

Lead me, Lord!

PROMULGATIONS

I receive Truth

The Holy Spirit is the Spirit of Truth

And He will guide me into all truth

For He speaks not of Himself

I receive wisdom

For the Lord withholds not wisdom, but gives
freely to whoever asks

I receive Knowledge and understanding

For the Spirit of the Lord is the Spirit of
knowledge and understanding

Therefore, I receive divine instructions

I overcome every confusion and aberration in Jesus Name

The Lord will Relocate my mind, my mental state and move me into the consciousness of the Truth in its entirety.

THANKSGIVING

Thank You Lord. I receive Your divine counsel and direction, for the steps of the righteous are ordered by You and you delight in them.

Jesus is the Way, the Truth and the Life. He shall be called Wonderful, *Counsellor*, The mighty God, The everlasting Father, The Prince of Peace.

PRAISE NOTES

_____

_____

_____

_____

_____

_____

_____

_____

_____

_____

_____

_____

Prayer if in Addiction

IT IS WRITTEN

The Spirit of the Lord GOD is upon me; because the LORD hath anointed me to preach good tidings unto the meek; he hath sent me to bind up the brokenhearted, <u>to proclaim liberty to the captives,</u> and the opening of the prison to *them that are* bound;' Isaiah 61:1.

And it shall come to pass in that day, *that* his burden shall be taken away from off thy shoulder, and his yoke from off thy neck, and the yoke shall be destroyed because of the anointing.' Isaiah 10:27.

MY PRAYER

Lord, I am not worthy to come to You, but on bended knees I come, through the Blood of Jesus Christ which was shed on the Cross of Calvary for my sins.

I know that Jesus came to set free, not to condemn,

To make whole, not to abandon

Thank You for Your mercies endure for ever

Draw me out of this pit

Destroy the yokes and break the chains of addiction over my life

Deliver me and cleanse me that I might praise and serve You alone.

Recreate in me, a clean heart.

Fill me with the hunger and thirst for your

righteousness.

Put new taste buds in me,

Holy desires, and a sound mind.

O Lord, give me a brand-new life, I ask in

Jesus Name.

Fill me with Your Holy Spirit, and let Your

healing power flow from Your presence, to me.

Wrap me round with Your holiness.

PROMULGATIONS

I am soaked deep in His presence.

I am immersed in the Blood of Jesus.

Christ has translated me from the kingdom of darkness into His marvellous light

Whosoever calls upon the Name of the Lord shall be saved

I denounce every alliance which might have been initiated consciously or unconsciously with the occult, alcohol, substances, any form of abuse. I denounce them today in the Wonderful Name of Jesus.

I break every unholy union

I cut off every tie and dependencies

I break bondages to sin and everything contrary to God's Word

I revenge every disobedience by the authority of God's Word

I reconnect myself to Christ; to holiness, to His righteousness, His Love, His Power and His Authority.

For this purpose, was the Son of God manifested that He might destroy every demonic operation and works of darkness

I am a new creation in Christ Jesus. Old things are passed _away_, behold, all things are become _New_.

'And he that sat upon the throne said, Behold, I make all things new.' Revelation 21:5a.

He who has begun a good work in me shall accomplish it in Jesus Name.

THANKSGIVING

I thank You Lord. In this, I will praise You. Because You have heard me, I will serve you. I will rejoice in Your salvation all the days of my life. Amen. My soul is escaped as a bird out of the snare of the fowlers: the snare is broken, and I am escaped! Psalm 124:7.

The Psalm of David

'Create in me a clean heart, O God; and renew a right spirit within me.

Cast me not away from thy presence; and take not thy holy spirit from me.

Restore unto me the joy of thy salvation; and uphold me *with thy* free spirit.'

Psalm 51:10 - 12.

Jesus *was* wounded for my transgressions, He *was* bruised for mine iniquities: the chastisement of my peace *was* upon Him; and with his stripes I am healed. Amen.

PRAISE NOTES

_____

_____

_____

_____

_____

_____

_____

_____

_____

_____

_____

_____

_____

_____

_____

Prayer when in bereavement

IT IS WRITTEN

'For his anger *endureth but* a moment; in his favour *is* life: weeping may endure for a night, but joy *cometh* in the morning.'   Psalm 30:5.

'To appoint unto them that mourn in Zion, to give unto them beauty for ashes, the oil of joy for mourning, the garment of praise for the spirit of heaviness; that they might be called trees of righteousness, the planting of the *LORD,* that he might be glorified.' *Isaiah* 61:3.

MY PRAYER

Lord, please fill this vacuum in my life with Your presence.

Carry me through this valley.

Open my eyes to Your unfailing love.

Fill my heart with your peace.

Reside in me Holy Spirit.

Help me to receive Your unfathomable love for me.

Holy Spirit, You are the Great Comforter. Be my Comforter.

Wipe away my tears Lord,

Turn my mourning into dancing and my sorrow into joy according to Your Word in Jesus Name. Amen.

Holy Spirit, You are welcome into my life, You are welcome in this place. Have Your Way.
Please bring Restoration and healing to my body, soul and spirit in Jesus Name.

PROMULGATIONS

I am whole

I am refreshed by the refreshing of the Living
waters

I receive beauty instead of ashes

The oil of joy instead of mourning,

I am no longer desolate nor forsaken

I am called by a new name; Hephzibah

I am God's delight

I shall be sought after

According to the revelations of Isaiah the
Prophet

My empty spaces are filled

And I shall say in my heart,

Where have these come from?

_W_ho hath brought forth these?

_B_ehold _I_ was left alone; these, where had they been?

THANKSGIVING

Lord J receive Your comfort. My hope is in Your Word, that we shall meet with our loved ones again, for all who die in Christ shall be resurrected with Him on the last day. Jesus said, that whoever believes in Him, though he (she) were dead, yet shall he (she) live: John 11:25. Thank You Lord for this Blessed Assurance. Amen.

Jesus is the Resurrection and the Life

PRAISE NOTES

Prayer if divorced or Separated

IT IS WRITTEN

Behold, the LORD hath proclaimed unto the end of the world, Say ye to the daughter of Zion, Behold, thy salvation cometh; behold, his reward *is* with him, and his work before him. Isaiah 62:11.

A bruised reed shall he not break, and the smoking flax shall he not quench: he shall bring forth judgment unto truth. Isaiah 42:3.

MY PRAYER

Lord, You are the Restorer.

You restore broken lives and broken dreams.

You bring recovery to the afflicted,

Hope to the despondent

Life to the desolate.

You are the Lily in the valley, the Rose in the

plains of Sharon.

Your Hands make whole.

My Father, my hope is in Your unfailing love.

My trust is in Your Divine Constancy.

Rebuild my life.

Put the broken pieces of my life together and heal

my wounded heart.

A smoking flax, Lord, You will not quench,
Whoever comes to You, You will in no wise cast out.
Please heal my brokenness and restore me.
Forgive my sins and any misdemeanours on my part.
Give to me a brand-new life
I pray in Jesus Name.

PROMULGATIONS

By God's healing power, J forget those things which are behind

J consider them not

J do not dwell on them

But J move forward to those things which are before

God will navigate my path and lead me into my divine destiny

He makes my crooked places straight and rough places smooth

He will reorder my steps

J disengage myself from every attachment to past failings and disappointments

My mountains have become a way

I have lost nothing

I am recovered,

I am restored, I am vindicated.

God has restored to me, the years that the locust hath eaten, the cankerworm, and the caterpillar, and the palmerworm. Amen.

And we know that all things work together for good to them that love God, to them who are the called according to His purpose.

Every bitterness, anger and resentment are washed away by the anointing of His presence.

THANKSGIVING

Thank You Lord for You have heard my prayers. I receive Victory over my accusers in the Name of Jesus. I receive Your healing. David said, 'When my father and my mother forsake me, then the LORD will take me up.' Psalm 27:10.

There is therefore now no condemnation to them which are in Christ Jesus, who walk not after the flesh, but after the Spirit. Amen.

PRAISE NOTES

_____

_____

_____

_____

_____

_____

_____

_____

_____

_____

_____

_____

_____

_____

_____

Prayer when Depression sets in

IT IS WRITTEN

Why art thou cast down, O my soul? and why art thou disquieted within me? hope thou in God: for J shall yet praise him, *who is* the health of my countenance, and my God.' Psalm 42:11.

'J cried by reason of mine affliction unto the LORD, and he heard me; out of the belly of hell cried J, *and* thou heardest my voice.' Jonah 2:2b.

MY PRAYERS

There is no mountain too high, that You cannot move,

No Valley too deep, You cannot reach.

If I made my bed in hell, You would still be there.

This is my consolation, that nothing can separate me from Your presence.

Yea though I journey through the Valley of the shadow of death, I will fear no evil, for You are with me.

You are Jehovah Shammah, the Lord is there, the Ever-present God.

Lift me out of the depth of this depression, *Catapult* me to newer heights of life and joy in *You.*

Fill me with *Your* overflowing joy, with *Your* unending joy, *Your* eternal joy, which no man can take away from me.

Refresh my mind of *Your* loving kindnesses to me.

Disengage me from oppressive spirits and suicidal thoughts.

Breathe Your breath of life on me, *Lord, I* pray in *Jesus Name.*

PROMULGATIONS

I have come to terms with the truth of God's salvation

Christ has liberated me from forces of oppression and wickednesses

I am loosed from every delusion and chains of the enemy

I speak the three words of creation; the heavenly language into my life as I declare:

Let there be

Let there be life

Let there be joy

Let there be a new mind, new thoughts

That I can do all things through Christ who strengthens me

That I shall not die but live to declare the goodness of the Lord in the land of the living. Amen.

For the Lord has put a new song into my mouth

And praise upon my lips

Not by might nor by power but the Spirit of God

I bring into extinction every demonic thought and utterance, and suggestions and inclinations

And I declare:

There shall not be any depression

There shall not be any regression

There shall not be any further manipulations of foul spirits and spirits of deception

There shall not be any further suicidal thoughts in Jesus Name. Amen.

But there shall be Synchronisation!

Peace, thoughts of life, thoughts of joy, in the Mighty Name of Jesus. Amen.

THANKSGIVING

I receive joy, the spirit of Praise instead of the spirit of Heaviness. I thank You Lord for a new and healthy disposition. You have healed me. I receive life and life

more abundantly in Jesus Name. I am delivered!

If Jesus shall make me free,
I shall be free Indeed! Amen!

PRAISE NOTES

_____
_____
_____
_____
_____
_____
_____
_____
_____
_____
_____
_____
_____
_____

Printed in Great Britain
by Amazon